PUT ON G♥D'S LOVE

Yvonne Lassley

AB ASPECT Books
www.ASPECTBooks.com

Copyright © 2013 Yvonne K. Lassley
ISBN-13: 978-1-4796-0090-8 (Paperback)
ISBN-13: 978-1-4796-0091-5 (ipad)
ISBN-13: 978-1-4796-0092-2 (Kindle Fire)
Library of Congress Control Number: 2013900608

His Holy Spirit
Is Joy, Peace, Goodness
And most of
All Love.

God sent His
Son to give
You a message.
Did you get it?

God sends His
Love to you
And yours.

God is with
You always.
Amen.

Where will you
Be when God
Comes for you?

God came to
Your rescue.
See you in
Heaven.

"Got God?"

1-800-Lord God

Got' R Done.
All
66
Chapters in
The Bible.

The Book is
Open.
Will your
Name
Be in it?

God's in the
Here
And now,
Are you?

The definition of
God
Is Love.
The definition of
Love
Is God.

One little, two little,
three little Angels
Four little, five little,
six little Angels
Seven little, eight little,
nine little Angels
Ten little Angels of God.

Do you see me now?

Do you hear me now?

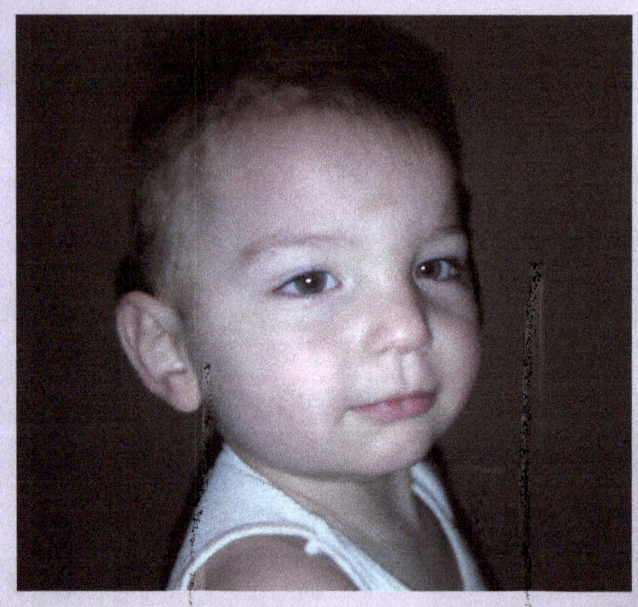

Stop looking over your Shoulder,
God is always in front of you.

God's time is forever,
Our time is short.

Instead of
Clapping,
Let's put our hands
Together and pray.

Jesus
Encourages
Sinners to
Unite for a
Short time
With Him eternally.

All people
Come
Together and
Pray for peace.

Time for the
Gloves to come
Off and get on
Our knees and
Pray for peace.

God's calling will you Answer?

Or will you be caught sleeping?

Connect the dots yet?

Fill in the pieces yet?

Noah did it two by two.

Teaser question
Of the day:
How many times
Will God forgive
You?

Instead of rolling
The dice or
Flipping a coin,
Why not take
A chance on God?

Life's got you down?
Look up and see God.

Gold...
Silver...
Pearls...
Oh my, looks like
Heaven.

On a roll, a roll up
Yonder,
Will you be there?

God is like Tide™,
He gets the
Tough sins out.

God is like bleach,
He makes you
White as snow.

I opened the door
And there He was,
Knock, knock,
Knocking on my heart.

God wants you!

Smile, I know
You want to!
I am because
God is
In my life.

I am blind,
But see
I am deaf,
But hear.
God is helping
Me with that.

Rip Van Winkle
Slept thru life,
What are you
Doing?
Wake up and live with
God.

All the little
Children knew
Who Jesus was,
Let's be a child.

Smile...
You're on
God's camera.

Are you missing something?
Got love?
Got peace?
Got faith?

Need God?

You're going on a trip!
You can't pack anything,
Everything is already there.
Where are you going?
1. Bermuda Triangle
2. Black Hole
3. Heaven

Answer is in the Bible

If you are going "there"
And "there" is here,
Where are you going?

Answer is in the Bible

A thief in the night,
Is as daylight as day,
Don't be caught off guard,
Watch and Pray.

Have you heard of any
Seas parting the waves lately?

Knock, knock,
Who's there?
God
God who?
God your Father.
If you let me in I will
Love you Forever.

I need you now,
Heaven is lonely
Without you in it.

What?
No way...
Jesus says he will forgive
Me of **All** my sins?

Have you read the Book?
It is a must read, it is about
Your future.

God is in town,
And He is looking for
A few sinners to save.
I Volunteered. Will You?

Don't work your
Way into Heaven.
Have a little Faith!

Jesus loves the little Children all over the World.

Jesus is the light of
The world,
So let us light
The world with
Him.
Pro Choice?
Pro Life?
Pro God!

God's the inventor.
No test tube needed.

God knows your story.
Do you know God's story?

Jesus is the Reason For any Season.

God's not going to be
Coming around the
Mountain,
He's going to be moving
Mountains.

Six days and six nights
Working for the man.
Seventh day I will rest
With my Maker.

There are no strike
Outs in Heaven,
Only home runs.

Pray, God is waiting
To hear from you.

God's recipe is simple.
First four commandments:
love Him,
Last six commandments:
love your neighbors as yourself.
Do all and live a happy life.

The question is not God,
The **answer** is God.

You've got 30 seconds to
Convince someone to give
Their life to Jesus.

Put on God's
Love
For Christ
Lives in You.

We invite you to view the complete
selection of titles we publish at:

www.AspectBooks.com

Scan with your mobile
device to go directly
to our website.

Please write or email us your praises, reactions, or
thoughts about this or any other book we publish at:

P.O. Box 954
Ringgold, GA 30736

info@AspectBooks.com

Aspect Books titles may be purchased in bulk for
educational, business, fund-raising, or sales promotional use.
For information, please e-mail:

BulkSales@AspectBooks.com

Finally, if you are interested in seeing
your own book in print, please contact us at:

publishing@AspectBooks.com

We would be happy to review your manuscript for free.

www.ingramcontent.com/pod-product-compliance
Lightning Source LLC
Chambersburg PA
CBHW082236170426
43196CB00041B/2830